650 | Holidays

Edited by Edward McCann

650 | WHERE WRITERS READ

Founder / Editor • Edward McCann
Executive Producer • Richard Kollath
Literary Ombudsman / Senior Editor • Steven Lewis
Chief of Operations • Jane Kaupp
Technical Advisor • Conrad Trautmann
Technical Advisor • Stephen Kaupp
Director of Communications • Gretchen Reed
Director of Photography • Kevin O'Connor
Videography/Photography • Sara Caldwell
Chief Audio Engineer • Jesse Chason
Copy Editor • Shelley Sadler Kenney
Copy Editor • Kathleen Stanley
Graphic Designer • Diane Fokas

Production Assistants
Robert and Lynn Dennison, Diane Fokas, Mackenzie Meeks,
Jackie Mercurio, Jessica Rao, and Brian Reagher

Advisory Committee
Rachel Aydt, Laura Shaine Cunningham, Angela Davis-Gardner,
Joseph Goodrich, Steven Lewis, David Masello, Honor Molloy,
Irene O'Garden, John Pielmeier, James Russek,
Angela Derecas Taylor, Julie Trelstad, and Gretchen Reed

"Thanksgiving dinners take eighteen hours to prepare.
They are consumed in twelve minutes.
Half-times take twelve minutes. This is not coincidence."

— *Erma Bombeck*

ABOUT 650

Holidays can set the stage for a delicious meal or a family drama. They can prompt memories of happy times, or present opportunities to create a new ones. This volume contains a sampling of diverse holiday experiences from a select group of talented writers featured and recorded at a live reading event in the Ossie Davis Theater at the New Rochelle Library in New York's Westchester County.

650 is a celebration of writing and the spoken word—a literary forum featuring two-page, 650-word personal stories that can be performed in five minutes. Our events at theaters, colleges, and libraries around the country are organized around single, broad topics that invite a range of expression, and recorded performances are added to a digital archive of writers reading their work aloud. The writers and their work receive additional exposure through podcasts, broadcasts, our YouTube channel, and in these printed volumes.

650 features graduate students and grandparents, first-timers and bestsellers. It's all about the writing, with an emphasis on craft. It's about the choice of one word over another, about the shape of sentences and paragraphs, the arc of a narrative, the poetry of a unique literary voice. If you love language and enjoy a good story, you've come to the right place. To submit your work or attend our shows, visit our website or Facebook page, and join our mailing list.

Please tell your friends about us, and **spread the word about the spoken word.**

Ed McCann

Edward McCann, Founder / Editor

READ650.COM
FACEBOOK.COM/READ650

CONTENTS

650 | Holidays

Edited by Edward McCann

KATHRYN MAYER

Kathryn Mayer is a potty-mouthed, sometimes cynical storyteller, humorist, and activist sharing life as she lives it in Newtown, Connecticut. She is a recent, reluctant inductee to AARP, the co-creator of two quasi-adults and two wannabees, and an aspiring writer with the rejections to prove it. She is sometimes funny on Instagram and Twitter as @KLMcopy, has invisible friends on Facebook, and writes about teenagers, midlife, social issues, feminism, and gun violence prevention.

A MEETING OF FIRSTS

Kathryn Mayer

Nothing says happy holidays like when the boy I lost my virginity to met the man I married one awkward Christmas Eve in my childhood home, while Karen Carpenter crooned to a house full of family and friends, and I got sloshed on embarrassment.

Ralph bounded into the celebration hugging an enormous poinsettia, peered through the flowers with big, brown bedroom eyes—not at me, but at my new husband. "Hold this, will ya buddy?" he said and thrust the plant at the spectator, slid off his Carhartt, tossing it on a chair erupting with coats and cats.

Ralph gave his nemesis an obligatory male head nod, not knowing who he was, not caring, took back his hostess gift and entered the room like Santa Clooney. He lifted my mother off the ground with a "Ho-ho-ho there, beautiful," while the poinsettia whacked my husband, Brad, in the head.

My mom was not at all surprised by this visitor of Christmas past.

I was.

1

When I first heard his voice I got butterflies, but not the good kind. The kind when you're almost in a head-on collision. I glared at my mother, still blushing from her favorite's hug.

"Really, mom?" A newlywed, I was with the entire family, and what-could-have-been stood face-to-face with what-was.

My mother used her "don't make a scene" voice: "Did I mention I saw Ralphie in town? Invited him for some eggnog for old times!" She fake-inhaled the fragrant-free flower, and whispered to me, "Still so handsome!"

She sauntered into the kitchen, the table full of holiday eats: bottles of booze, silver bowl of eggnog, shrimp, cookies and cakes, and a traditional Christmas ham. She pushed them all back and placed the poinsettia front and center, its leaves dipping into the eggnog, then crying drops of Jack Daniels onto the cheese platter.

I felt its pain.

Aunts and uncles, oddball cousins, and friends hushed at the commotion. They whispered: some wondering who the newcomer was, and some knowing full well my sexual history.

"HA! HA! HA! Ralph, you old son-of-a-bitch!" My dad's laugh could wake the dead. A lifetime ago, his booming voice had thrown this man-boy out of the house more than once.

My father, two-fisting ham sandwiches, his big belly shaking like a bowl full of, well, you know, swung one arm around Ralph's neck, whipped the other around my husband, pulling them both in for a dual headlock. Crumbs from my dad's bushy Santa beard fell onto receding hairlines, ham sandwiches leaking mustard under both of their chins.

"Look at you!" he bellowed, freeing Ralph, but only slightly loosening his grip on his son-in-law. "How the hell are ya? You two fellas sure have a helluva lot in common, don't they Kath! But Ralphie, this gotta hurt!" Mouth full of ham, he sent a congratulatory nod to the son-in-law tucked safely under his arm.

I laughed. A little. My husband smirked, proudly, from under the ham fist. Ralph laughed, albeit awkwardly.

Then the spiked nog kicked in, and my parents, my past, and my present all fell into a new party game: stories about me. Kathy. Kate. Yes, she still cursed like a mother-trucker, collected stray animals and lonely people, bit her nails until they bled, was wicked, and wickedly funny.

When I sneezed rapid fire in threes—those cats—and rubbed my nose in tiny circles, my past and my present said "stop" in unison and proceeded to discuss my other unattractive habits. Does she still do this? What about that?

Before I knew it, I was listening and laughing. Two strangers becoming fast friends, and I recognized myself in their same but very different stories, and realized, that awkward Christmas Eve, that who I am now isn't so different from who I was then.

And for once—actually twice—in my life, I had chosen wisely and didn't regret a thing.

JOHN PIELMEIER

John Pielmeier began his career with the play and movie Agnes of God. Since then, he has had three more plays mounted on Broadway and twenty-five film, television movies and miniseries produced. Most recently he has written and acted in the internationally successful limited series, The Pillars of the Earth, and his stage adaptation of The Exorcist premiered in the West End in 2017 and is bound for Broadway. His first novel, Hook's Tale, was published by Scribner in July 2017. In between, he has received the Humanitas Award (plus two nominations), five Writers' Guild Award nominations, a Gemini Award (plus a nomination), an Edgar Award, the Camie Award, a Christopher Award, and been nominated for the Emmy Award (three times) and the Golden Globe Award. He is married to writer Irene O'Garden and makes his home in upstate New York.

THE INTOXICATION OF INDEPENDENCE

John Pielmeier

I've never been fond of Independence Day—maybe because it was the first day I ever got drunk—independently, sickeningly drunk. I was seven.

Let me explain.

My paternal grandfather was the meanest man in Altoona, Pennsylvania—that's how everyone described him. Everyone. He beat his children, he cheated on his wife, he worked as little as possible, and every penny she earned he spent on cars. He hated African-Americans, Italian-Americans, Polish-Americans, Irish-Americans, and probably dogs and babies too. One of his eight children cursed him in his coffin: he was mean even when he was dead. When he was alive, he was often drunk.

His children, as a consequence, pretty much avoided alcohol. My father drank one beer a week with his Saturday dinner, and he would occasionally pour a thimbleful into a Kraft Cheese glass and allow me a sip. I loved it.

One July fourth, shortly after receiving a plaster statue of the child Jesus for being the brightest and politest boy in first grade, I went with my father to a family reunion. My mother stayed home with my four-year-old sister; it was just Daddy and me. He sat at a picnic table chatting with adult cousins I had no interest in, and being the good father he was, he allowed me to do whatever the hell I wanted. What I most wanted was sitting on ice in a big tin tub nearby. Being the bright polite award-winning boy that I was, I went to my father and asked: "Daddy, can I have some beer?"

"Sure," he said and went back to his family chat.

I took out a bottle, popped the cap, and drank. It was cool and effervescent and the perfect thirst-quencher on a hot holiday afternoon. If they had allowed seven-year-old boys to serve as spokespersons for Pabst Blue Ribbon, I would have been a star! That beer was so good—how good?— So good I just had to have another.

About a quarter of the way through bottle number two, I noticed the world was moving in a remarkable way, kind of—I don't know— tipping on its side. I'd seen comedian drunks on TV stumbling and slurring their words and, recognizing these symptoms, I staggered to my father and announced, brightly and politely:

"Daddy, I'm drunk!"

He evinced paternal concern. "Sure you are. Very funny. Go play."

I didn't. I just sat in the grass and stared at a Roman candle someone had lit. It was the most beautiful thing ever! It was a preview of heaven.

Hell arrived when, driving home post-picnic, we hit a rabbit crossing the road. I heard the thump and felt the bump and I burst into tears.

"Daddy, you killed it! It was going home to its wife and babies and you killed it!"

I sobbed and sobbed and sobbed. And then I passed out.

What happened next I don't really remember, but I was later filled in by a trustworthy eyewitness: my mother. She and Daddy, having both grown up with acrimonious parents who fought in front of the children, always held their disagreements in our basement garage, away from us kids. Not this night. This night, with my sister asleep and me in a Pilsner coma, my mother let my father know her exact feelings about his bringing home a drunken child — right there in our front hallway.

But it isn't the July Fourth fireworks in our home that I remember, or even the one-and-a-half bottles of beer; it's the remarkable beauty of that Roman candle burning in the grass: the intoxication that came — that comes — from independence.

PAULA FUNG

Paula Fung lives in a charming neighborhood just north of New York City, with her husband, three daughters, and their dog Boomer. She produces a show on public access television, Rye Views, the local reading series Writes & Bites in Rye, and writes personal essays on the things she knows, which are, in no particular order, cooking, sailing, and family life. Her work has been published on the blog, Sailing Anarchy.

KITCHEN BINDERS

Paula Fung

Always a fan of school supplies, I have a trove of recipes in my white binder labeled "Holidays," which sits on my kitchen shelf. Each recipe is enclosed in a plastic sleeve, sections tabbed in chronological order of the celebrations.

New Year's brunch recipes are followed by one for a Valentine cheesecake, knife-swirled with a chocolate heart, then a flourless chocolate walnut cake, then a graph paper diagram of an Easter bunny with tremendous ears, my template for Easter dessert. Right behind them is my Rosh Hashanah brisket recipe, an old standby of Heinz Chili Sauce, Coca Cola, and Lipton Onion Soup. Then a doodled list of the bagels and cheeses I order each year from the one local bagel store that understands, after many years, that Yom Kippur actually is an event here in Rye. My foolproof potato latkes come next, and closing out the year is the one for chocolate and coconut pecan pie, a true Christmas stunner.

At my wedding shower, guests were asked to bring their favorite recipes written on index cards. The index cards were added to a photo book and this became my first binder. That book contains my mom's chocolate mousse recipe, my cousin's potato salad made with hard-boiled eggs, and my sister in law's caramel "blondies." The binder collection grew as we had children and my interest in cooking expanded along with the size of my family.

With millions of recipes easily available online, reaching for my binders feels a bit primitive. Many of the recipes are handwritten, some cut from The New York Times or ripped out of magazines while waiting for doctors. Tucked into the pages are lists of invitees, some already gone from our lives. Dishes served are listed and often annotated "honey mustard sauce too bland—NEEDS BALSAMIC;" "sweet potato kugel—BIG HIT." And as I flip through one binder or another, on each slippery page, my heart floods with sweet memories of hosting holiday dinners with my husband at my side; he checks the turkey while I refill wine glasses in the living room, taking a moment to watch the kids playing Risk and Mancala marbles spilling onto the floor.

I am Jewish, my husband is Chinese, raised in the Presbyterian Church. Every Christmas, I bring my mothers' chocolate mousse cake to my in-law's. Each Chanukah, my husband fries the latkes at my parents' house. On Chinese New Year, I make a beef and broccoli dish and long noodles to signify the hope of a long life.

I sometimes worry that my husband and I have not done a proper job of religious education with our three daughters. I never wanted to choose or make them choose, as if our traditions were polar opposites, instead of integral parts that give our five-subject family its unique flavor.

If we chose Jewish, our kids would have missed the thrill of walking around Jones Farm in Connecticut with a rusty saw searching for the perfect tree to cut down for our cleared-out corner of the living room. If we chose Christian, they would miss the excitement of the first tastes of wine at the Passover table and then the marvelous discovery a few years later when they realize that Manischewitz is not really a good example of the magic of wine. If they were not proficient with chopsticks and didn't know how to bite a tiny hole into soup dumplings, they would not know how to suck out the luscious velvety flavor. A recipe for those dumplings, by the way, can be found in a white binder on my kitchen shelf.

ANN LEVIN

Ann Levin is a freelance writer and editor in New York City. She worked for The Associated Press (AP) for twenty years as a reporter and editor, most of the time based in Manhattan. Before that, she reported for papers in Texas and San Diego. Since leaving the AP in 2009, she has worked as an editor for the United Nations Population Fund and Columbia University, written articles for the *AARP Bulletin* and other publications, and contributed book reviews to the AP. She lives on New York City's Upper East Side with her husband, Stan Honda, a photographer.

HOLIDAYS OPTIONAL

Ann Levin

My father hated holidays. He thought they were an invention of the greeting card industry, aided and abetted by shopping mall operators, to sell people a bunch of stuff they didn't need.

"If you want anything, I'll buy it for you," he'd say. But we were children, impervious to reason, and so, for at least a few years, especially in elementary school, he and my mother went along with the gift-buying program. In a low-key sort of way.

On Hanukkah, we got practical things like socks and sweaters—but only on the first night. For "Show and Tell Day" at school, when you had to bring in your best Christmas present, the gentile girls showed off their Easy-Bake ovens. I brought in my latest itchy sweater.

After my mother died, we found letters my father wrote to her, agonizing over what to get for her birthday. "Dearest Sal," one began. "I just came from Allison's"— that was the name of the newsstand on Main Street— "and the cards were so banal I couldn't bear to send you one."

"I just want you to know," he continued, "that I know you're having a birthday on the twenty-ninth—but more than that, that every day of your life is a great and important day for me. I feel tremendous gratitude for your existence and am very proud you're my wife. I really don't know what I'd do without you. I love you dearly, Len."

If that sounds a little over the top, that's because my father knew that holidays—especially birthdays— – meant everything to my mother. In that respect, she was like the New York City Transportation Department, which lists thirty-four legal and religious holidays when alternate side parking rules are suspended. She would have been all in for all of them.

Luckily, both my parents were gourmets, so he happily went along with her inclination to throw a feast every chance she got. On the Fourth of July, she hauled out her red, white and blue tablecloths. On Hanukkah, the dreidel napkin rings. In late December, twinkling lights and pine boughs. And if the Steelers made it to the Super Bowl, then she went to the party store and bought black and gold crepe streamers.

Growing up with one parent who adored holidays and another who disdained them, I had to decide for myself which, if any, rituals to follow. As a Jew, I had no inclination to celebrate Christian holidays. As an atheist, I had no attachment to Jewish ones either. Then I married a nonbelieving Buddhist, who was indifferent to all three. Since we didn't have kids, we had no obligation to pass on our amorphous heritage. In other words, we were off the hook. Holidays were strictly optional.

For a number of years, Stan and I exchanged token birthday presents, until we reached the age when the bigger problem was how to get rid of all our stuff. That left Valentine's Day, Thanksgiving, New Year's and our anniversary.

Our anniversary was easy. Neither one of us could remember it. We'd originally picked a date to get married that was convenient for our relatives to come to New York to witness the ceremony at City Hall. Then we took the Number Six train uptown and watched a later stage of the three-week Tour de France. So we're pretty sure it's in late July, and that's close enough for us.

Both of us agreed with my dad about Valentine's Day—it's just a manufactured event designed to peddle candy, flowers, and heart-shaped tchotchkes.

That still left two biggies: Thanksgiving and New Year's. But when a secular Jew marries a secular Japanese American, the solution's a no-brainer. We go to the one place in town that symbolizes for us the festive spirit of the holidays.

We go to Chinatown for dim sum.

LYNN EDELSON

Lynn Edelson is a special educator and family trainer in the New York State Early Intervention Program. She is the mother of two grown sons, a writer and a musician, and is fairly certain neither one will ever buy her a beach house. For the past five years, she has studied memoir at The Writing Institute at Sarah Lawrence College. Though she has often been accused of writing poetry, she is currently at work on a collection of short stories. In May 2016, her essay, *Heart Monitor*, was selected to be part of the New York City *Listen To Your Mother* show. Lynn lives in the Hudson Valley with her husband, Michael Principe, and Sadie (aka The Bad Dog of Brewster).

INVIOLABLE RULES
OF THE UNIVERSE

Lynn Edelson

My husband and I grew up in the same neighborhood, so we both knew the rules about what a house is supposed to look like during the holidays: large, incandescent rainbow-colored bulbs, shining brightly for all to see. Tastefully done, of course. A simple string along the porch railing, and perhaps one underneath the gutters framing the front of the house. Lights that greet us as we come up the walkway, reminding us that, despite the gray days of late fall, Christmas is almost here.

Those lights are just enough to stir my Jewish heart, but never over the top.

Our two sons always knew they had a full ticket to Christmas and Santa always came to their house. They never asked, "Does Santa really bring presents to Jewish kids?" or, "Where's the menorah?"

They asked, "When is Dad putting up the lights?"

Most people in the northeast put their lights up right after Thanksgiving. The weather is still relatively mild. Not my husband.

"Today?" I ask him on a sunny day with no wind.

"It's not cold enough," he replies.

Clearly, there are rules. Any self-respecting Catholic knows you have to suffer a bit, like all those Christian martyrs.

We usually bring our tree home two weeks before Christmas. The ornaments are a mix of store-bought and homemade, and we all know the history of each of them by heart.

"Didn't we get this at the Times Square store when we were first living together?" I ask while holding up a small wooden blue car that resembled our 1969 VW bug. My husband smiles and nods his head.

The first Christmas we shared in our new apartment, we had nothing to hang on the skinny tree. Our budget was tight, but we splurged on two strings of the large incandescent rainbow bulbs and a few wooden ornaments that we found for halfprice.

"Why does he have more ornaments with his name on them?" the younger child asks (he is now in his thirties).

"Because they loved me more," the older child replies with a grin.

"Who wants to put the tinsel on?" I ask, as they both reach for a handful. My husband shakes his head, knowing he'll have to redo those glimmering strands, because, well, there are rules. Only one piece at a time.

"Don't put them on like Artie," he warns and we all laugh.

Artie is our best friend from the old neighborhood. He takes small clumps of tinsel as he drinks his cocktail, and though he begins with single threads, by the end he is usually in the middle of a political discussion and simply tosses the rest wherever there is a bald spot.

When the tinsel is done, we usually step outside and admire the tiny farmhouse, lit up inside and out, with the tree in her glory, framed in the window.

We'd had a good run for years. I followed the rules. He followed the rules.

Until last year.

Until my husband went shopping without me.

On that cold and blustery fall day, he carried the new lights up the ladder and tacked them up beneath the gutters.

Blue LED lights. Elegant lights. Sophisticated lights. But not my lights. My lights were still a tousled mess in a carton in the garage.

"Don't they look good?" he asked as he climbed down the ladder.

"Where are the other lights?" I asked.

"They're over there," he said, pointing at the small Douglas fir propped up outside on the porch—an afterthought draped in my large, multi-colored incandescent bulbs.

"But where are the rest?" I asked.

"I wanted to try these this year," he said, avoiding my eyes.

We both knew he had broken the covenant. And we both knew I wouldn't insist he climb back up that ladder to switch them out. But I steeled myself as he snuck a hopeful look in my direction and thought, "Never again."

JOHN GREDLER

John Gredler, poet and memoirist, is a frequent contributor to 650 who's been writing in notebooks and journals for most of his adult life. He honed his craft at the Writing Institute at Sarah Lawrence College, Bella Villa Writers, 125, and the Terzo Piano Workshops. A recipient of the 2014 Kathryn Gurfein Fellowship from The Writing Institute at Sarah Lawrence College, John's work has been published in *Atticus Review, Fictionique, Narratively, Dan's Papers, Westchester Review,* and *Talking Writing.* John lives and writes in Tuckahoe, New York.

CHRISTMAS POLAROID

John Gredler

In the Polaroid, my mother and older sister are in front of the Christmas tree. It's a fake tree so it must be after Mom married my stepfather, Tom. Jeanne kneels on the floor with her hands pressed together, tucked between her thighs. She is looking up and over toward the stairs. Caught out of her usual guarded appearance, her open face is disarming. Beautiful even.

My mother sits on the couch smiling for the camera. She wears a powder blue pants suit. Her hair a dyed brunette bob.

I am in the background sitting at the dining room table. A plate of food is off to the side. My right hand holding a mug of tea, my left hand is propping up my head, elbow leaning on the table. I am looking down, bleary eyed and morose.

The night before I'd gone with a group of friends to the Village Inn to celebrate Christmas Eve. It was a dismal space. Dark walls, a black vinyl bumper running the length of the bar. The low-ceilinged room with Formica-topped metal tables and dim lighting. But full of people it felt like the place to be. It was crowded when we arrived. I was with Jimmy Meyers and Barry Bizzard. We squeezed up to the packed bar and ordered beers. Jimmy ordered shots all around. Jack Daniels. I was never a drinker of whiskey or bourbon, certainly not straight up. No one would have cared if I drank it or not. But I cared. I wanted to be one of the boys. Bourbon was what men drank.

After I managed a rough couple of shots the others started going down easier. This had never happened for me before and it made me drink more. Chased with more beers.

It must have been two or three in the morning. when we left. We got into Jimmy's car, his father's big Cadillac Sedan DeVille . He pulled a U-turn right in front of the bar, the screeching tires burning rubber the whole time. Then we were flying down Larchmont Avenue. I was yelling at him to slow down but he just laughed and went faster. So I started laughing too.

Somehow Jimmy got us to Barry's place without getting pulled over or going off the road. It is here that my memory ends. Barry told me that I smoked a joint with him but didn't say a word. "You just sat there. Your eyes were real glassy. Then you were gone."

I don't know how I made it home; I must've walked the half mile to my street. The next thing I remember is waking up and puking into a shirt I grabbed from the chair next to my bed. My brother told me later he had ironed that shirt to wear on Christmas morning.

I was sick a long time. Vomiting until I was down to dry heaving. All the while I could hear the Christmas music and the sounds of presents being opened downstairs. I knew too that they could hear me.

By the time I managed to shower and make my way down they had finished with the Christmas meal. Everyone avoided looking at me. I went to the kitchen to make a cup of tea. There was nowhere to hide in our small house so I sat at the dining room table. After a while my mother got up and fixed me a plate of turkey with stuffing and mashed potatoes with gravy. My favorite meal. I pushed it away.

It must have been my brother who came down the stairs and surprised Jeanne with the flash of the Polaroid camera, her face radiant with wonder. Like Mary, the mother of God, kneeling in awe before the newborn Jesus.

JENNIFER RAWLINGS

Jennifer Rawlings is an award winning writer and performer who's appeared on Comedy Central, CMT, PBS, FOX, VH-1, A&E, CNN, HLN, Current, *The Joy Behar Show*, and two recent TEDx talks. Named one of the "21 Leaders of the 21st Century" by Women's E News, she's performed in over 350 military shows in such countries as Iraq and Afghanistan. Her directorial debut—*Forgotten Voices: Women in Bosnia*—received critical acclaim, has screened at film festivals worldwide, and is part of the curriculum at several universities. She's written books, for television and film, and for numerous publications including *The New York Times* and *Reader's Digest*. In addition to cooking, cleaning, and driving in circles, Jennifer—the mother of five—is currently finishing a new book and touring her solo show, *I Only Smoke in War Zones*.

AN ALASKAN AULD LANG SYNE

Jennifer Rawlings

New Year's Eve: a time to sip champagne and sing "Auld Lang Syne." Unless, of course you're a stand-up comic. Then New Year's Eve is a workday.

Let me tell you about New Year's Eve in Alaska. Have you ever been to Alaska? It's north of Oregon, north of Washington, and north of one of my favorite parts of the United States: Canada.

Alaska has a lot more men than women; it's all guns, moose and drinking. It's basically a bar that was given statehood.

The first time I worked in Alaska I was a young comedian in a seven hundred-seat venue. There were three acts on the bill; I was the middle act, following a dance troupe that opened the show.

I showed up early, notes in hand, wearing a black blazer, jeans, not too much cleavage, and closed-toe shoes. Then the dance troupe showed up, with stilettos, sequins, feathers, garters, and thongs.

I would be doing my, "Hi I'm from Kansas" clean comedy act AFTER a dance troupe called "The Bush Company" performed. They were strippers!

The next time I performed in Alaska was on New Year's Eve, at a twenty thousand-seat arena. I was touring with the country band, Lonestar.

This was a big deal. Playing an arena show on New Year's Eve— even for a comedian—is a nice payday. But I'd heard the promoter of this show was a weasel, and I was worried about getting paid. My agent said, "Don't fret. Your money will be at sound check."

Sound check came, sound check went. No check.

I was stressing. I had five kids who all liked to eat and I needed that money. I tried to call my agent, then my manager, but it was New Year's Eve and they were nowhere to be found. Desperate, I call Lonestar's road manager to see if they got paid. They did. "No problem," he added, "I'll make sure your check will be in your dressing room when you get to the venue tonight."

I got there. No check.

I saw the promoter and asked him.

"Would you believe it?" he replied, "I gave the last check to Lonestar, the cash box didn't show up... (blah, blah blah); I promise I will FedEx you a check on Monday."

I'd been contracted to do forty-five minutes of stand-up before Lonestar came on, and if I don't go on, I don't get paid.

I know this guy will use any excuse to not pay me, and I must hold up every part of our agreement. forty-five minutes, not forty-four and not forty-six.

Onstage, it was brutal. The sound mix got changed from sound check and only the people on the floor could hear me. I saw people passed out or throwing up, and a heckler screamed "Take it off lady!" I wondered if it was someone from The Bush Company.

Finally, my time in hell came to an end; at 11:45 when I walked off stage, the crowd was going wild screaming for Lonestar; I was sweating, but I hadn't breached my contract.

In the wings, the band members and promoter gave me high fives. Then Richie, the lead singer, looked directly at me and—over the stomping feet and roar of the crowd—screamed a question:

"Have you been paid yet?"

"No."

"Well," Richie said to the promoter, "We're not going on stage until Jennifer has been paid."

11:48—"I'm out of checks, the cash box isn't here!"

11:49—The rafters were shaking as twenty thousand people stomped and screamed, "Lonestar, Lonestar!"

11:50—The promoter ran to his office, returning with a bag of money.

"Are you sure you'll be okay carrying all this cash?"

"Cash is fine," I told him.

And at midnight, as Lonestar sang "Auld Lang Syne," I swayed along backstage with crisp hundred dollar bills safely tucked inside my bra.

I learned that from the strippers.

ANTHONY MURPHY

Anthony Murphy is originally from Lancashire, England, and now lives in Yonkers, New York. He is an associate producer of the spoken word event, Rimes of the Ancient Mariner, in downtown Manhattan. Nominated for a Pushcart Prize 2017 for work that appeared in *The Westchester Review*, he's the author of the mixed-up book of poems and prose, *Scoppetry*, available on demand. His graphic poem, "Liberty Takes a Break," is available at choice bookstores. Murphy curates the online time travel blog *Where The Wurms Play Rugby*, a space for tales of place and time.

HOLIDAY IN BODRUM, TURKEY

Anthony Murphy

We were on holiday. We needed some kind of fix, even though we had just gotten back together. We needed to take ourselves out of our old routines, out of our old landlocked lives, to see.

We went to West Turkey, a tourist destination for a mix of Europeans who play it safe in the Mediterranean. In our hotel everybody seemed to be from Yorkshire. Turns out that Doncaster's Robin Hood Airport had direct flights to Bodrum. We had flown in from London and yet here we were with a cocktail of British Northerners. It's not exactly an exclusive club, and it's one you might want to escape from, but when in Rome... Olivia, being from Kent, wasn't happy. I had a new bunch of drinking buddies.

One morning after, I find out that Olivia has booked us on a trip. We are to take a boat. I am still drunk as she urges me up. No time for coffee. A taxi takes us down to the boat and we board with a bunch of others. My eyes aren't working yet, but it's a big boat. There must be fifty of us. We are a little crammed in.

Soon we can look at the natural green and blue beauty of the land instead of having to ogle each other through sunglasses. The skipper anchors and we see a swimming opportunity. There are other boats and there are whoops of delight as brave ones jump. We gently drop into the warmth and tranquility of the sea.

Then over at the cliffs, there is a splash as someone dives. Wow! And as we look up, there are willing divers on top of an outcrop, and as we follow with our eyes back down, there is a crawling trail of white people in swimsuits.

Olivia, she whoops too! She is a strong swimmer and freestyles off towards the base cliff jumping point. I struggle to keep up and am a little tired as I clamber out after her onto land. She urges me on up the rocky path to where we think the locals are congregating. Some white men are walking back down by us, saying "No way!"

When we get up there, we realize that most people are just watching. Sure, they have their swimming gear on, but they aren't brave enough to leap. It's a freak show. The trail is just tourists steadily swimming from boats to have a look. We have only seen one person jump. Olivia has no such qualms. She urges on, takes her step and leaps feet first over the rocks into a God knows what plunge. I see her bikini bum narrowly miss a scrape before she disappears. I daren't look over. The group of young, local lads gasp and cheer. Shit! They all look at me now. I can't walk back down. So... I take five steps back and then surge forward and leap after her.

I try to keep my body straight. It takes a while, and where is the water? I look down to see where the water is and that's when it hits me in the face.

I sink. I don't even try to get back to the surface, it just happens. Eventually there is air.

"Are you all right?" Olivia asks. She is laughing. It must have looked funny because she can't stop laughing. One of my eyeballs has been pushed backwards into my skull. I feel sick. There are a couple of others there, still in the deep pool.

"We saw you, that was bad. Are you okay? It was the worst entry."
I gasp a bit and I find it difficult to swim, or tread water. I have no
energy to even curse them. Olivia swims ahead, she's chuckling. I
float on my back and look at the blue sky and wonder on the lack of
clouds. It's beautiful.

ELLEN NENNER

The progression of **Ellen Nenner**'s life has taken her from music student at the High School of Music & Art, to piano student at The Juilliard School, to an economics/philosophy major at Mount Holyoke College, and finally to an MA in Urban Planning from the New School. Formerly a writer and editor at the consulting behemoth McKinsey & Company, Ellen has attended writing workshops at the Fine Arts Work Center in Provincetown, Massachusetts. She's a trustee on the board of MasterVoices, a not-for-profit performing arts institution that believes that the human voice is the world's most powerful instrument. Music is Ellen's great passion and she has found a profound connection between telling stories through music and telling stories through the written word. She is currently working on a non-fiction book of connected essays and short stories.

THE STURGEON FROM THE BACK

Ellen Nenner

My family subscribes to a well-worn culinary course of action on Yom Kippur, the most solemn religious fast of the Jewish year. We begin with a festive meal: oatmeal-colored matzo balls reposing in bright yellow chicken soup enlivened with dill, braised-for-hours beef brisket paired with broccoli mornay, and rice pilaf enriched with caramelized onions. Pears turned crimson by their long bath in spiced red wine complete the meal. Hors d'oeuvres are never given a thought since dinner is invariably a race against sunset by which time we must be in synagogue.

For the next twenty-five hours we pray, atone, and fast until the Rabbi blows the shofar signaling the Day of Atonement is over and we are free to break the fast. I prepare for this celebratory meal days earlier when I make the run from my home in Queens to Russ & Daughters, the renowned appetizing store in lower Manhattan. I arrive close to nine in the morning and quickly take a number from the ticket dispenser. I know I will have at least sixty minutes to revisit photographs of four generations of ownership displayed on the walls and delight in the bounty before me: great sides of smoked salmon—Irish, Scotch, Norwegian, Western Nova—and little chubs, big whitefish, satiny sable, exotic caviars, pickled herrings, cream cheese schmears, babkas, and bagels crowned with seeds. As I wait, I nod hello to familiar faces from last year's culinary pilgrimage.

Time passes. The number currently being served signals that I can inch closer to the carving station of my favorite server. If I'm lucky, she will be free when it's my turn.

"Ninety-three," Marta's voice rings out.

Yes!!!

A brief smile, good to see you, how've you been, then on to business. "Let's start with the fish. How many people?"

"Ten. I'm debating between the Scotch salmon and the Irish this year."

"I'll give you a taste of each."

"The Scotch," I finally tell her after savoring its subtle combination of smoke, salt and fat.

Marta picks up a long, thin carving knife, her other gloved hand anchoring the fish. No surgeon has a sharper scalpel or a better feel for the angle at which to make the incision and the pressure required to produce the desired result—slice after slice of translucent salmon. The scale registers a pound.

"Is that it?" she asks.

"Not yet. I want some of the sturgeon from the back."

She smiles, maneuvers past her colleagues, turns right at the end of the display cases, and enters the dimly lit storeroom. Minutes later she wends her way back, cradling a brown paper package. "How many slices?"

"Eight or nine. It's just for me."

She unwraps the sturgeon and carefully cuts the white flesh "on-the-bias." As the fish adjusts to room temperature, droplets of fat ooze onto the knife, lubricating the blade for the next slice.

She offers me a generous sample. The meat is mild, slightly sweet with a hint of smokiness. It has an unctuous quality but there is no suggestion of greasiness. It is supremely moist and exceptionally delicious. At almost sixty dollars a pound, I am grateful that no one else in the family reveres the sturgeon from the back as I do. The nine slices will cost about thirty dollars but I legitimize my lavish indulgence as a once-a-year purchase.

We arrive home from synagogue to the smell of fresh coffee and erupt into the dining room. Taking pride of place on the damask-covered table is a curious wooden platter shaped like an elongated fish, its head and tail rendered in sculptured brass. It carries the best of the best from Russ & Daughters. The sturgeon, however, sits alone at my elbow—isolated from the main culinary offerings. We fill our plates, drink to the New Year, and set the inevitable political discourse in motion.

ANGELA DERECAS TAYLOR

Angela Derecas Taylor writes about food and family dysfunction. A descendant of Greek and Italian immigrants, she was born and raised in a family restaurant business in 1960s Greenwich Village. Angela has traveled extensively, working for more than twenty years in the food and beverage industry, until her volunteerism and advocacy led to a mid-life career change into her current role as the executive aide to the mayor of New Rochelle. She has been published in The *Westchester Review* and is a featured storyteller with Read650, Pros(e) of Pie, and The Creative Breath. She has also taken the stage at The Moth story slams in New York City. Visit Angela's website — FoodWineAndWords.com — for stories, events, and recipes.

THE TURKEY SHOOT

Angela Derecas Taylor

I was five years old and it was the start of the holiday season. My parents separated when I was four months old, I'd never spent a single holiday with both of my parents, and the visitation agreement allowed for Dad to have me every other Sunday. Who would get me on holidays was left to my parents to work out on their own.

One Sunday before Thanksgiving, Dad planned to bring me to a turkey shoot, an annual outing he attended with his sister, my Aunt Sophie, and her husband, Uncle Jim. Getting a bulls-eye meant winning a Thanksgiving turkey.

"She's too young," Mom said. "This is an adult thing."

"She'll be fine," Dad said. "Sophie will keep an eye on her."

"Last time you brought this kid back from Jersey, she had a broken arm and head lice!" Mom yelled. "Why can't you just take her to the park and get her an ice cream?"

I was the only child at the event, roaming freely among preoccupied adults. Adults with rifles. Shooting at targets.

All I cared about was winning a turkey. I was sure I could do it.

"Daddy, can I shoot?"

"No, you're too little."

I begged him. Please. Let me shoot. I can do it. You're so mean! Let me shoot. Please! I kept pestering until I wore him down. Finally, Dad lifted me onto a stool so that we stood, more or less, at the same height. With my back nestled against his chest, we extended our arms together along the cold steel barrel of the rifle. Dad raised the rifle to take aim, helping wrap my tiny forefinger and thumb around the trigger before placing his fingers on top, the rest of his big, strong hand enveloping mine.

My body tingled with anticipation. I knew we were going to win a turkey, and that would show Mommy how great Daddy was. Then maybe she'd let me go with him on Thanksgiving Day—and maybe stop saying all those mean things about him.

Dad and I were cheek to cheek as he nudged my head aside to look through the viewfinder. Then he allowed me to look, and I squeezed one eye closed like I'd watched him do, staring hard at the bullseye in the center of the target.

"Ready to win a turkey?" he asked.

"Yes, Daddy!"

I took a deep breath and held it as we squeezed the trigger.

BAM!

The blast of the shotgun caused a powerful kickback. The gunstock nailed me right between the eyes. I screamed in shock and pain as blood from a deep gash flowed down my face and into my mouth. People yelled that my dad was an idiot for letting me shoot and my Uncle Jim, who'd been a medic in the Korean War, took over triage.

"A butterfly's good for now," he said. "She probably needs a stitch to avoid a nasty scar. Let's get her to the emergency room."

"Nah," Dad said. "She'll be fine. But look at this!"

Dad held up the target paper showing the hole my bullet made right at the very edge of the still-intact bullseye. "My best damn shot of the day."

I moved the ice pack away and raised my throbbing head, squinting through swelling eyelids at the paper target.

"Did we win the turkey, Daddy?"

"No. The hump wouldn't give it to us," Dad replied, disgusted. He held my chin and studied my face, turning it from side to side. "Hmm. Your mother's gonna love this."

"I'm sorry, Daddy," I blubbered, wiping the blood, tears, and snot with my sleeve.

That year, I spent Thanksgiving with my mom.

LESLIE MIGNAULT

Leslie Mignault is an elementary school-based speech/language pathologist who has also worked as a waitress, secretary, cake decorator, script reader, garage sale organizer, film production assistant, story editor, and tutor. She has a larger than average number of graduate degrees because she couldn't make up her mind. Her favorite punctuation mark, hands down, is the parentheses. She lives in New Rochelle, New York with her family.

HAVE YOURSELVES A MERRY

Leslie Mignault

The winter I was five, my parents and I drove to Connecticut to buy a puppy my mom had found in the newspaper. The dog seemed fine to me, but what really got my attention was the family's Christmas tree. Smothered with tinsel, encircled by a moving train, smelling of oranges and vanilla, it dominated their living room.

We did not celebrate Christmas, and I'd never met anyone who did. Up until this moment, I had thought of Christmas and its trappings—the elves, the caroling, the reindeers—as something strictly for television; a show with the same level of reality as, say, Leave it to Beaver or Mister Ed. I had no idea that real people acted that way.

On the drive home, as the new puppy slept on the seat next to me, I tried to talk to my parents about what I now realized was a gross inequity.

"Why do they have a Christmas tree?" I asked.

"Because they're Christian," my father answered. "It's their holiday."

"Is it an American holiday?" I asked.

My father snorted. "You could say that," he replied.

My mother cut in. "They celebrate Christmas; we celebrate Hanukkah," she told me, in a tone that suggested the discussion was over. "It's exactly the same thing."

Flash forward twenty years. It's December, and I am meeting my boyfriend's mother for the first time. There's a tasteful white wreath on the door of her South Orange Tudor. I'm told she has a question about the holidays only I can answer. Although she lives within commuting distance to New York City, she has apparently never had this kind of unfettered access to a Jewish person before.

"What I don't understand is this," she finally asks me, in the tone you'd reserve for wondering what lies beyond the edges of the known universe. "What, exactly, do you do on Christmas Day?"

"Oh, that's easy," I tell her. "Eat Chinese food and go to the movies."

And I do. That Christmas Day, I take myself to a matinee. It has snowed all night and Broadway is silent and clean. I trudge downtown to the Paris Theatre and join a small crowd waiting for the first show. An older couple walks over to Sixth Avenue and returns with coffees for all of us. A guy with a beard hands out warm banana bread.

The theatre opens and I head up to the balcony. As the lights dim and the velvet curtains part, I put my boots up on the railing and lean back. The guy with the beard is to my right, smiling in the dark. These people are my people. I have never felt so keenly that I belong somewhere as I do at this moment.

Flash forward another twenty years. It's December, and my husband and our son are in our cozy suburban living room, decorating a Christmas tree with ornaments gathered from our life together. Behind them, in the bay window, menorah candles glow.

My son pulls a homemade ornament from the box and hands

it to his father. It's an old one: a smiling self-portrait in a lopsided frame made of Popsicle sticks. My husband hangs it near the top, and for a moment they look at it together.

With a pang, I understand that this child, repository of my hopes and fears, inheritor of the blood of survivors, has feelings about Christmas that are—unlike mine—joyful and unalloyed. But isn't that what it means to raise a child? At a certain point, doesn't he stop being one of us and become one of himself?

My husband laughs at something and pulls our son into his arms. I smell fresh pinesap and burning beeswax—and the lingering, oniony odor of latkes. These are my people. And this is where I belong.

STEVEN LEWIS

Steven Lewis, Literary Ombudsman for 650, is a columnist at *Talking Writing*, and a member of the Sarah Lawrence College Writing Institute faculty. A longtime freelancer, his work has been published in *The New York Times, The Washington Post, Christian Science Monitor,* the *Los Angeles Times, Ploughshares, Spirituality & Health* and others. His novels include *Take This and Loving Violet,* both from Codhill Press, and Finishing Line Press published Steve's poetry chapbook, *If I Die Before You Wake.* His backlist includes *Zen and the Art of Fatherhood, The ABCs of Real Family Values, The Complete Guide for the Anxious Groom,* and *Fear and Loathing of Boca Raton (a Hippie's Guide to the New Sixties).* He divides his time between his writing space in New Paltz, NY and Hatteras Island, NC.

PASSING OVER PASSOVER

Steven Lewis

Last spring, like a daffodil shoot breaking through winter soil, I recalled with unexpected affection the Seders my family held when I was a boy ... cousins running around Aunt Betty's tiny Hollis basement, Uncle Mac's Great Neck backyard, aproned mothers cooking brisket in steamy kitchens, the hearty cigarette laughter of dads as they shorthanded and shorter-handed the Pesach service.

At first, I figured that since I'm not religious and the fond memories occurred around my seventy-second birthday, it was probably just another incidence of an old man waxing sentimental. Nevertheless, hoping my enthusiasm was not a sign of incipient dementia, I figured it was time to learn something beyond my Encyclopedia Britannica knowledge of the Jews' liberation from slavery in Egypt. I knew about the more famous plagues God imposed upon the Egyptian people (frogs, lice, boils, locusts), though others (water into blood, mixture of wild animals, diseased livestock, hail, darkness) were a revelation to me. However, it wasn't until number ten, the death of every Egyptian first-born son, that I stopped breathing.

The clouds parted, the bush in my brain burst into flames … and I suddenly understood that Passover isn't simply about my forebears' deliverance from persecution, which would be a real cause for celebration and a big party with aunts cooking, uncles laughing, cousins running all around, everyone eating brisket and kishke. It is also about frogs, lice, boils, locusts, the slaughter of lambs and … and … and … the sacrifice of innocent little boys.

Talk about a matzoh ball that sinks to the bottom of the tureen with a thud, cracking the bowl, soup pouring out all over the holiday table.

Can there be joy in that brand of carnage?

No heavenly answer was forthcoming.

But I received a second "Aha!" moment a few days later while reading the daily disheartening reports in my morning Times… Jihad in the Middle East, genocides in Africa, Christian persecution in Russia and China, Anti-Semitism in … well, everywhere. Which was when I realized that the Passover story is not all that different than the stories that have emerged from every religion on the face of the earth throughout human history—and that at the heart of all those supposedly sacred narratives is the notion that one tribe's survival is somehow enabled by the suffering or destruction of others, almost all of whom are innocents.

Which momentarily allowed this Jew to understand why Jesus had to die for our sins.

Which was when I heard a rustling from a neighboring bush in my brain and, like Abraham, imagined a ram caught by its horns (Genesis 22:13) … and in that moment considered the possibility that the sacrifice of innocent boys was not God's will. Or plan. Maybe the passage was simply a creation of God's fallible creations, the human stain on the hallowed universe that makes religion a battlefield instead of a sanctuary.

Which inadvertently led me to Twitter and God@
TheTweetOfGod, who tweeted, "You're the worst species I ever
created, and I made 3,500 different cockroaches."

Which in turn took me by the hand and led me to Chanukah
and the miracle of the lights ... or, much closer to home, the
absurd Lewis Power Chanukah (eight days in one itty bitty candle-
lit dinner) ... and the unmitigated joy of watching this tribe of
Jewlattos, *QuadJewns*, and, lo and behold, non-Jews, having a big
ass party with aunts and uncles cooking, cousins running around
giggling and breaking things, everyone mumbling a prayer only I
understand, then eating gloppy good food, and finally topping it all
off with gambling in the form of Chanukah Bingo without Boils and
cutthroat Dreidel, no diseased livestock allowed.

And even if there are tears shed, no one has to die.

SAMANTHA WOODRUFF

Samantha Woodruff holds a BA in Eastern European History from Wesleyan University and an MBA from NYU's Stern School of Business. She spent most of her career on the business side of Viacom's Kids and Family Network Group, where she oversaw strategy, business development, and consumer research for Nickelodeon and a host of other brands. After becoming a mom and moving to the suburbs of Manhattan, Sam left corporate America to focus on her passions—her children, yoga and writing. Sam's full-time job is now taking care of her two kids—ages seven and nine. In her free moments, she also teaches yoga and takes classes at The Writing Institute at Sarah Lawrence. She is working on her first novel (and may be doing so forever) and writing essays that try to take a lighter look at the life of a former type-A executive turned suburban mom.

GOOD TIDINGS

Samantha Woodruff

My Ancestry.com DNA profile: 98% Jew.

I was bat mitzvahed in a pink, puffy-sleeved Laura Ashley dress, and my mellifluous haftorah made the congregation cry. I am Jewish with no wiggle room, except in my faith, which is "skeptical" at best. And my love of Christmas, which is limitless.

When I married a Presbyterian, Christmas became mine; I started listening to Christmas carols non-stop while cooking Thanksgiving, and reluctantly turned them off when my husband cried "uncle" on New Year's Day. I cultivated a vast stable of décor ranging from two Christmas trees—the "family" one decorated with gems like my husband's 30-year-old, now-one-legged skiing reindeer and heavily-glittered popsicle stick snowflakes that my kids made; and the "formal" one with glass Kurt Adler nutcrackers and a professionally-tied tree-top ribbon—to Mamacita, a stuffed Chihuahua in a pom-pom fringed sombrero who waves her paws while singing "Donde Esta Santa Claus?"

I hand wrap every, single, gift.

Every year I say I'll do less. Every year I don't. I can't help it;

I'm a type-A perfectionist, and a Christmas junkie.

As with all addictions, it turns out that Christmas, too, has a dark underbelly—the pressure of holiday cards. Holiday cards aren't advertised on TV or featured in poignant movies; yet in WASP culture they, like a dry martini at five, are part of life.

My first card was a snapshot of my baby daughter captioned: "Merry Everything" (I felt any overt reference to "Christ" crossed a line.) I labeled, stuffed, sealed, stamped and mailed 120 envelopes to arrive before Christmas. It was a Hanukkah miracle. And Sam Greene from New Jersey transitioned into Samantha Woodruff (soon-to-be-from Connecticut).

Then, I actually moved to the suburbs. Here, holiday cards were a competitive sport. The apotheosis of suburban wifedom. Everybody sent one, and each was more elaborate than the next: handmounted photographs, pre-strung ornaments, and tri-fold collages with pithy descriptions of the year's milestones. Receiving cards was equally important—if you got less than five every day of December, you were clearly a total loser.

I was frightened. Overwhelmed.

Galvanized.

I dressed my kids in thematic outfits for professional photos (the only acceptable option if you didn't capture a perfect moment on your summer in Nantucket). I expanded my list to include new acquaintances. I hand wrote "XO" on cards for my friends, so they would know that I knew that I knew them. I couldn't bear to hand address the 250 plus envelopes—the coup de grace of a true card maven—but I did change the font on my labels to look like handwriting. Despite my near mastery of the Game of Cards, every year I enjoyed it less.

I wish I could tell you that I chose to opt-out of this annual activity that was sucking all the joy out of Christmas. But I didn't.

Instead, my marriage hit an un-Christmas-like rough patch and, as the holidays approached, real life supplanted cards. Out of time and enthusiasm, I posted a snapshot of my kids on Facebook captioned: "Happy Holidays, this is my card."

I expected to be cast out of my club's annual Brunch with Santa, barred from all Junior League events. Instead, I became a social media goddess. Flooded with likes, loves and commendations for my bravery.

Two years and zero cards later, I can proudly say that I still have friends and I've even been asked to chair a committee at my kids' school. This season, while your Instagram feed sucks valuable hours from your endless list of holiday to-dos, keep an eye out for my kids and obscenely large collection of singing stuffed animals. That will be my card.

JACK O'CONNELL

Jack O'Connell is a New York City native presently living on Long Island with his wife, Margaret. He is a working actor with extensive film credits including *Doubt, Big Night, Inside Llewyn Davis, The Paper, God's Pocket, The Quitter, Brazzaville Teenager, Everyday People, The Yards,* and others. Numerous TV credits include *Mad Men, Nurse Jackie,* and *Vinyl,* and Jack is currently seen on the Emmy Award-winning Netflix hit *The Marvelous Mrs. Maisel,* playing Jerry, the elevator operator. Jack is a member of Artists Without Walls.

SONGS OF THE SEASON

Jack O'Connell

I am in my grandmother's parlor. It is the early 1950s and my WW II uncles are sitting around the piano as the singing becomes louder and louder. My young cousins and I laugh when Uncle Walter puts down his Chesterfield and drinks and dons a "Rudolph the Red-Nosed Reindeer" mask. Eventually, everyone joins in singing "I'll Be Home for Christmas."

"Adeste Fidelis": We are seated in the grade school auditorium at Our Lady of Perpetual Help in Richmond Hill, Queens ... and how jealous am I that my sister knows all the words in Latin while I can barely stumble through the English version of "O Come All Ye Faithful".

"It's Beginning to Look a Lot Like Christmas": I am with mother and brother window gazing under the L train on Jamaica Avenue. It is 1953 and I want the Rawlings three-finger mitt, Stan Musial model with red Rawlings label stitched on back of hand strap. There it is in Davega's window.

"God Rest Ye Merry Gentlemen": I am seated in an overstuffed armchair in my Aunt Minnie's apartment. In front of me on the thirteen-inch Philco, the yule log slowly burns on WPIX, channel eleven. She offers me some chocolate chip cookies she baked as the yule log was burning. I fall asleep in chair.

"Santa Claus Is Coming to Town": We descend the stairs of our framed row house on 127th St. The Lionel train circles the trunk of our Christmas tree and a white milk truck picks up milk cans from a platform. I lie down next to tracks to watch closely. "Don't let the tinsel fall on the track," says Mom. "It could start a fire!"

"Auld Lang Syne"—Old Long Since": Guy Lombardo and his Royal Canadians are coming to us live from the ballroom of the Hotel Roosevelt in the heart of Manhattan. I am sitting at the top of the stairs, listening. Stella and John are in front of the television, plate of creamed herring, pumpernickel bread, red onion, limburger cheese and cold cuts. Brother Carmen Lombardo croons into the microphone, "It's Later Than You Think" as middle-aged couples sway away. Dad asks Mom, "Can you spot Gus and Eunice on the floor? They are there every year, Gus gets the tickets in October." Mom says, "They can do that... with no kids!"

"Silent Night": My father is on a ladder, hand painting the Nativity scene on a picture window in our new home on Long Island. It takes days to complete this folksy rendition. I remain silent in school when other students joke and laugh that we brought "Queens" out to their special 1950s Long Island.

"White Christmas" and I'm in the army: Sitting in a phone booth on Christmas day, relatives take turns saying "hello." Sounds of gaiety and laughter exit the receiver and I picture them all around the table. My father is last to speak and says, "Keep your chin up."

"Silver Bells- It's Christmas Time in the City": It's 1976 and I'm the father of four young ones as we drive into "Fun City" to see The Tree. We stroll up Fifth Avenue, take a walk through FAO Schwartz, mainly for the bathroom, and head back down Fifth on the other side. Chestnuts are roasting away in the cold December air; I barely have enough "jingles" for Pepsi and pretzels. Suddenly a horse-drawn carriage stops next to us. A handsome woman, holding the reins, asks us if we would like a ride. "Can't afford one," I answer, to which she replies, "I didn't ask if you could afford anything." I think I'm dreaming as I lift the children onto her blanketed seats. Kids squeal in delight as we clop down Fifth Avenue and the driver turns to say in her Dublin accent, "Happy Christmas."

ACKNOWLEDGMENTS

In addition to the contributors to this volume, we thank the **New Rochelle Council on the Arts** for its generous support of Read650, and for stimulating and encouraging the study and presentation of the performing and fine arts. Throughout the year, NRCA sponsors many exhibitions, theatrical productions, dance recitals, film screenings, lectures, and concert series. **NewRochelleArts.org**

We thank **The New Rochelle Public Library** for making their beautiful Ossie Davis Theater available to us. The library offers a comprehensive collection that includes retrospective and current materials; up-to-date technology by which information can be accessed; and a wide range of community services and programs tailored to a diverse audience.
NRPL.org

We're grateful to **Nancy Manocherian's** *the cell*, which supported 650 at its inception. A twenty-first century salon in the heart of New York City, their mission is to support the arts and to incubate new works, and the cell made its beautiful performance space available to 650 as we were finding our way. The cell: To mine the mind, pierce the heart, and awaken the soul. **TheCellTheatre.org**

A very special thanks to **Sheila Gilday** of Gilday Creative for her invaluable help in assembling this volume on short notice. Gilday Creative is a digitally forward independent website and graphic design agency based in the Hudson Valley that crafts strategies and design experiences to make things better.
gildaycreative.com/

READ650.COM

INFO @READ650.COM
FACEBOOK.COM/READ650